The Morning After

MICHAEL MARTINEZ

Copyright © 2018 Michael Martinez
All rights reserved
First Edition

PAGE PUBLISHING, INC.
New York, NY

First originally published by Page Publishing, Inc. 2018

ISBN 978-1-64350-456-8 (Paperback)
ISBN 978-1-64350-457-5 (Digital)

Printed in the United States of America

Thank you Michelle.

"all in all, I learned a lesson from it though, you never see it coming, you just get it to see go" – Aubrey Drake Graham "fireworks"

We swam in a sea of loneliness drowning
in the deepest love that would never be

She gave me all her trust and told me
all her secrets, she opened her heart and
what I found was a thousand pieces

I think this fling did more harm than good but something deep inside always knew it would

Those heels weren't made for walking but that's what they'll do, it'd be the last thing you feel, when she walks all over you

Sleeping has me closer to my dreams and
it's the only place I can see you now

I'm desperately craving you in so many ways

I wanted to catch up but got
caught up in the moment

You pushed me knowing I was afraid to fall, I stayed high for a reason, I didn't want to put my heart through another lonely winter season

We live in a generation of being good enough to sleep with but not being good enough to wake up too

She's cutting ties and said you're hanging on by a string, she wants to tie the knot but that's not my thing

I remember feeling weak and for that moment that I could touch your face through my six inch screen, I felt complete…ly miserable

Stayed up late looking at these stars wondering…
if I'll fall as fast as they do someday

I tried to get a hold of you but my hands were tied to someone else's bed, now you know how I felt when you used to leave me on read

Look at you and your new fling, you think he's an angel but even the devil once had wings

I don't even know what I want
out of love anymore…

I threw our love away, I'd rather recycle women like you, what's the point of making love to someone true when i can have more than two …

Please forgive me and don't run away, my mouth only vomits words cause my heart doesn't know how to beg you to stay

You waited for his call for what seemed like eternity and in that time you felt your heart break a million times

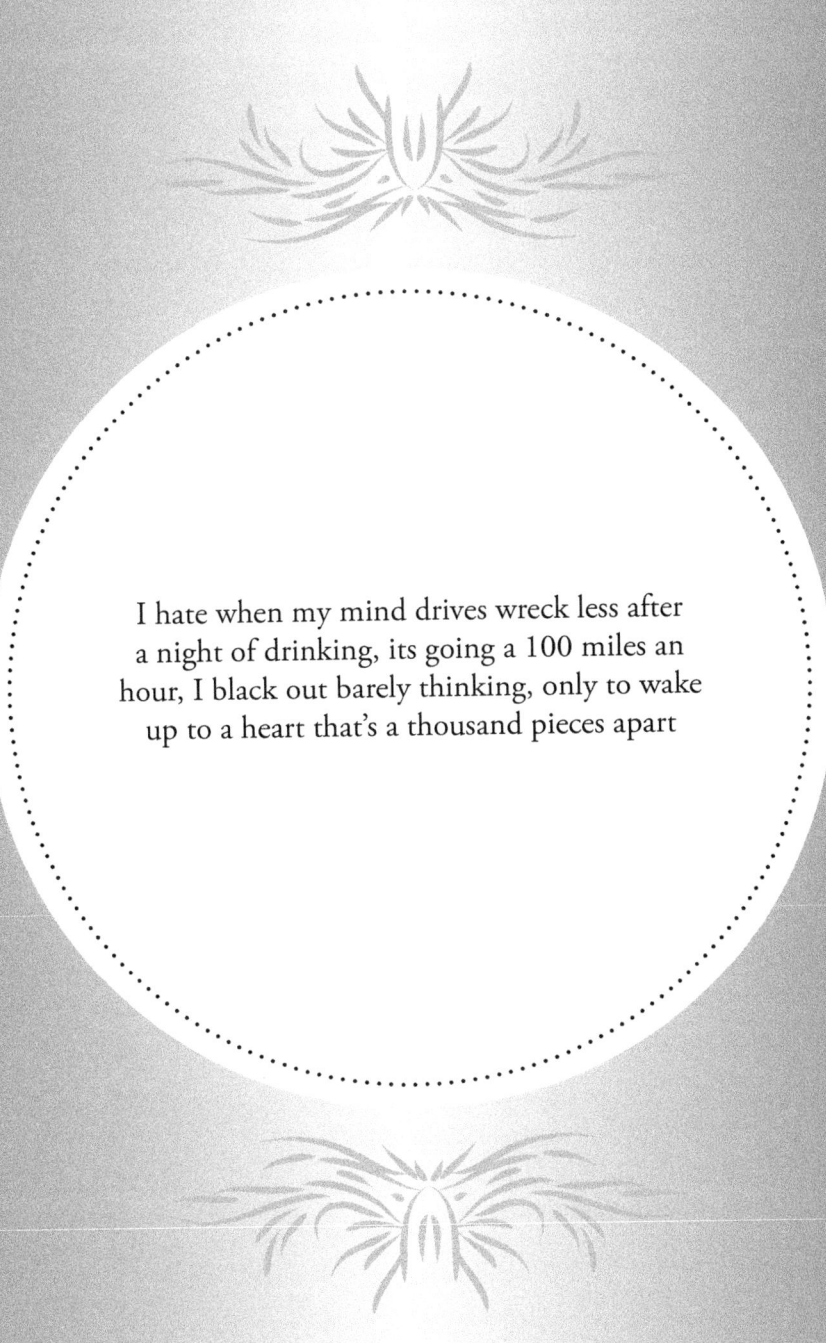

I hate when my mind drives wreck less after a night of drinking, its going a 100 miles an hour, I black out barely thinking, only to wake up to a heart that's a thousand pieces apart

You want a way out, but every exit just leads you back to the beginning, when things were fine but somewhere down the line, you realize that you never really loved him, you just didn't know what it was like to be alone

She knew I'd be the death of her but I never believed her until I took her breathe away

You say I never make time for you but this knife in my back says otherwise, I even let you cut pieces of my heart so we'd spend less time apart

If you're not in my dreams you'll always be in my heart, even if the distance between us is worlds apart

Last chance a thousand lives ago but somehow
I still managed to take her life and soul

I never stayed in a place that just
didn't feel like home, whether it was in
someone heart or someone bed

The sun coming up as I'm coming down since you're not around

We're back and forth like tug a war, the tension is high and your patience is thin, you broke my heart when you aimed for my chin

She burned bridges so he had no way to chase her, it was her way of setting him free

Love conquers all, well as I lay here in ruin, trying to piece back together everything that is ruined

I see the hell in hello but no good in goodbyes
this is what dating is like when you're a good guy

You stole my heart and planned your escape, you just couldn't do life with me, now I'll spend my nights behind bars

Your hand on the trigger... I wish you'd pull it and blow the thought of us out of my head

Mirror mirror on the wall why am I so quick
to fall or am I doomed to never find love
at all mirror mirror on the wall please stop
showing me the loneliest of them all

You're the love of my life… I can't believe I died a thousand times before you and if you go, I know I'll die a thousand more

Round after round, I hear that deafening sound, no ring, last call, I had with you such a brawl, too bad for me I lost it all, the bartender threw in the towel … I had enough

Not having closure, has me looking from the outside in, don't know who you are anymore but still wondering how you been

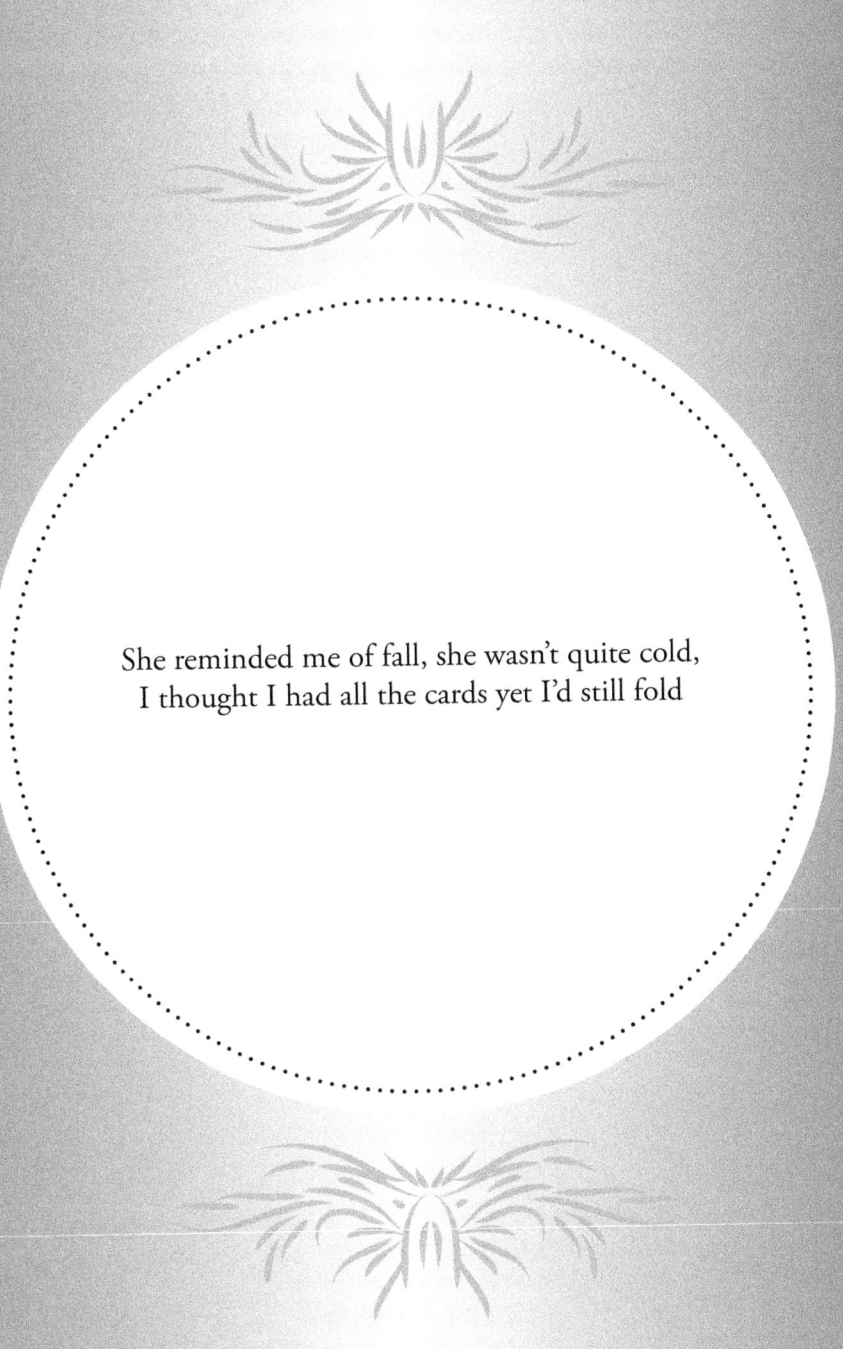

She reminded me of fall, she wasn't quite cold,
I thought I had all the cards yet I'd still fold

I'm afraid of commitment and when someone gets to close I turn into a ghost, a memory that lingers, I'm so childish for waving my middle fingers

I'm afraid of things that go bump in the night
but when the bass drops, my heart stops and this
ghost from the past is right next to me, knees weak
from this pill peak our love so old its antique

she had wings but he kept her down so
long she forgot what it was like to fly

I find myself missing women I had no problem letting go but lose myself on the thought of why I was first to go

We created magic together and she loved me for that but hated me for my disappearing act

I think I only broke hearts in hopes of
being able to piece mine back together,
but the more I broke the more I broke

I sold my soul for rhythm and now I'm cursed with the blues sorry if I'm late I just couldn't find my blue suede shoes

We had relationship goals but got stopped
at the one yard line, she had to many fans
screaming from the side line to ever be mine

I thought this game was going to be one
on one but she had a card up her sleeve
she had been cheating since day one

She told me I was her rock but how was I
supposed to know holding her down would
cause her to drown with a love so deep

All is fair in love and war so that
peace of mind is out the door

I'm intoxicated by the thought of you
but the cold reality is that it's over and
its worse than my hang over

Your smile is intoxicating I could be hung over in bed with you all day

I have multiple women and this multiple choice has me wanting to choose all the above but if I get this wrong then who knows how long I'll be stuck with miss wrong

She had a lot to say but never got herself
to send those messages, she just bottled
them up with her emotions and put them
on the shelf with her love potions

Closed lipped kisses always told something more, she kept the passion hidden like skeletons behind closet doors

Her mom said to keep space between
us, you can't trust boys from mars

Somewhere in my broken heart are
pieces of you and I, trying to pick up
where we left off has it difficult when my
fingers feel like they've been cut off

I didn't mean to go ghost on you but the skeletons in your closet had a way of haunting me even when you weren't around

She was from Venus and I was from mars, this long-distance relationship left us nothing but scars

I begged her to stay… as my silence
pushed her further away

She said please don't come and go, but I was gone
just there for show, said anything to just cum and go

She put up with his shit so long when her knees hit the ground it sounded like a tree hit the ground but with no one around does a broken heart make a sound

My west Texas rose, I didn't know much blue beside the sky, until I met her, now these blues are all I write, I did her wrong, I fought with myself to make it right, now my west Texas roses only comes out for neon light

Cross my heart and hope to die, write these poems, while you live a lie, stuck a needle but it wasn't in my eye, I blame myself because I didn't try

Your heels are high but your
hopes were another story

I knew she was a criminal when she stole
my heart and my peace of mind

I blame my drunken mind and clumsy hands for breaking your heart and if my mouth wasn't tired from running I would have said sorry from the start

Buried deep in her chest is a heart of gold, should I be foolish and walk away or should I be bold

She said I was the one that got away,
she gave me a 1000 reasons to stay but I
had this planned since the first day

I hate that you choose his bed over mine, after each fight and say you're staying at your friends for the night but you'd do anything just to feel right and he'd say anything to have you for another night

Girls night out always ended in a house that wasn't a home, with a morning that wasn't good and with some body that wasn't somebody

She loved the way the whiskey kissed her
lips, the burning reminded her of him

I share the same fear as dr. Frankenstein when he created his monster ... I'm responsible for the 5'2 devil with no heart that eats men and steals sweaters

This relationship was one sided like the
coins that I flipped into a wishing well,
wishing well or wishing you well

I'm trying to win her over but she hates to lose,
she's playing games with me and some other dudes

When he left her, she proved to
him but most importantly
to herself, that a broken heart can still
beat under neon stars and hip hop

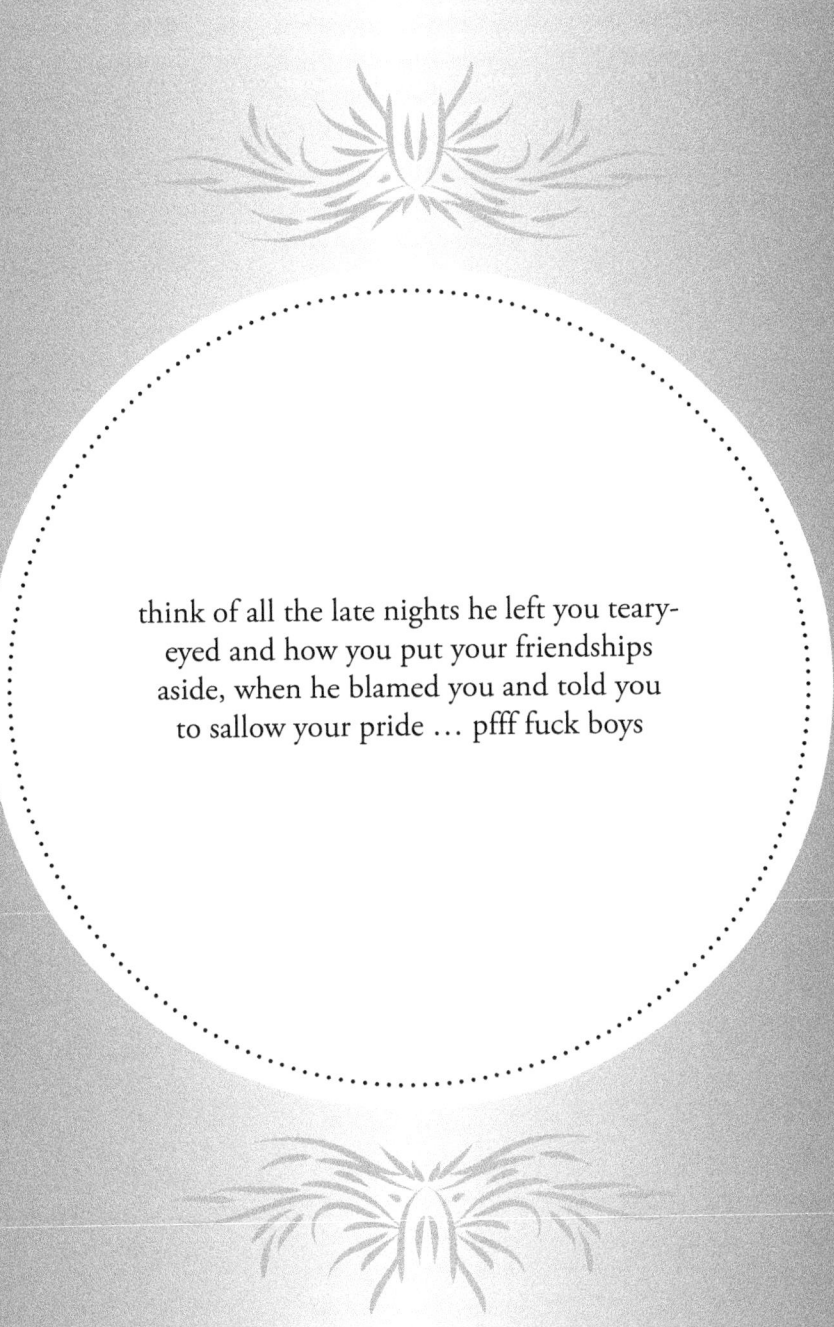

think of all the late nights he left you teary-eyed and how you put your friendships aside, when he blamed you and told you to sallow your pride ... pfff fuck boys

I hate when you say someday
like its apart of the week

Sunday to Sunday to someday but someday never comes and one day turns to 365, should I count on you or count down the days to keep this hope alive

I hate to be up front but I hate being on the side, I thought you wanted to be my bonnie so much for me being your clyde

She kept the devil in the details
and point down to her heels

She wanted me on the side because she could never fall back on whoever stood behind her

The feeling of pain inside me is what keeps her alive, it might be killing me but I can't risk losing her forever

It was 12 days till Christmas and I must have wrote your name a 100 times on my wish list and I know I need to let go, I just want to kiss you one more time under mistletoe

I wanna give you my heart, the only thing is…
its missing a few parts, I'm just letting you
know from the start, before it all falls apart

I didn't know giving someone your heart would be the death of you, now I understand why zombies crave brains

I asked "where you've been" but you respond
with a simple grin, guess somethings are better
left unsaid, not much to do but go back to bed

He broke promises and trust but that still wasn't enough, he stole her heart and sold her soul, now she just a shell of someone I used to know

Love comes at a price, that everyone is afraid to pay,
we'd rather walk away and save it for a rainy day

How are we supposed to look out for each other
when you have your eyes on someone else

I think roses are red, like they want to stop
you from being blue, no time for sweet
talk, that's why I only text you at 2

She said I got charm but she doesn't
know how unlucky she's about to be,
if only she knew the real me

She gave me the green light go over but these roses are so red they got me wanting to stop and pull over

She's so high off these pills and other drugs, she thinks that she's falling but he knows that this isn't love

She never gave me the time of day, but we'd talk 24/7, 365, I still don't understand how someone can make you feel more dead than alive

She said "we're moving too fast, the room is spinning out of control, I'm spilling my emotions, heart and soul."

I'm posted up like polaroids on your wall, you said you'd meet me for dinner but its already last call

She was more embarrassed to fall in love, than to fall in heels. when I asked why, she said "it's easier to get up from the ground"

Pour your heart of gold out, cast it into a ring, for someone that means everything

I think being in love had me on a high,
I keep popping pills, cause with someone
new, I can't feel it, even when I try

He played with fire and burned there home,
now she's a ghost that roams different sheets

She playing with his mind, I guess she lost her heart in the last game but boys don't play fair, she asked for truth when she should have dared

We kept the distance like two pen pals
and it's just the same, we only write each
other cause were not right for each other,
but I still wonder who's to blame

My friend would always tell me
"pay women no mind."
But all this attention I gave them came at a cost

I climbed the walls that you put up, I
didn't think twice, I jumped and I fell so
fast I forgot that I was made of glass

I told her my love was deeper than the ocean and more loving than the sky, she said "with some much blue in your life, it's amazing you still try."

I knew she was priceless but he made
her feel worthless, that's what it's like
to be in love with your best friend

I never realized how childish I was, until playing with women became much more fun than playing video games

He made it seem like he was heaven sent but that fallen angel seems to only drag you through hell

Found these old letters from my ex, everything from a to z, I just never found L.O.V.E.

I think I've been hanging out with these broken women, just to have an idea of what it feels like to be complete but just end up completely miserable

She lived in my sweaters, I regret being so cold, now I live in our sheets, where dreams of her never get old

You look dead tired or maybe just
dead looking from the inside out

I want to work it out but I can't get myself
to lift the weight off my shoulders

She's trying to find the one but she's been with everyone now she's left without anyone

I remember when she packed my bags and said she needs me to go, she got me a one-way guilt trip, when she had the problem with blow

I never wanted to look you in your eyes
for fear my heart would turn to stone

You want me to open up but my ex lost the key, you can pick all you want but that's just the hennessy

The way you sugar coated everything made me sick to my stomach, I should have known better… when everything you promised was hard to swallow

I'm jumping into relationships head
first but halfhearted. Forgive me

I can't wait till he takes you apart, I hope he starts with your heart and leaves your eyes so you can see him walk out your life stay lonely for me… let your heart beat slow… break eye contact, so no one can know, forever mine, never yours… stay lonely for me

I did you dirty but you're the one washing your hands, I'm trying to cut these girls off but they got other plans, I'll beg you for a second chance... look me in my eyes even if It's just a glance

I swear my nights seem to drag like the cigarette you share with your lover, you're undercover while I'm under covers

I don't know what's gotten into me, Is it the Hennessy or the memories… the thought of being single forever has me feeling like I'm my own worst enemy

I thought you were my ride or die but all you did
was hide and lie, almost choked and died when
I swallowed my pride and gave us a second try

It's hard to find the words when you leave
me in the dark, I'm trying to flip the switch
but that's like driving a car in park

You know my plate full but you still
keep feeding me your bullshit

I'm treading open water drowning in the thought of you, the thought of us.

I hold it in but you said "you hold me back," when
I had your back and not stabbed your back, heard
you drink till all you see is black and want me back

She called him every name in the book when she grabbed his phone and had herself a little look

I hope she makes it home, drunk driving asking what time he'll be home, she popped pills while her friend lectures her on the phone with that tired tone

I know I'm rock but the weight of my guilt
is sinking us fast as we fall deeper in love

She went the extra mile for me
especially when I pushed her away

Her playlist had some deep cuts... I couldn't believe it, it's no wonder when someone told her they loved her. she'd never repeat it

How useless can I be if you still use me, confuse me, lose me but still 2 a.m. choose me

my sleepless nights got me day dreaming about
us I just can't bare another nightmare about you

With my mind so cloudy it's just a matter
of time till the tears run down my face

Why do I always feel so alone, when my cell phone going suicidal blowing up at 2am with messages like "hey" and "are you home," I want something real but fuck it up when I answer my phone "hey, I'm alone"

I hope you spend Valentine's Day alone, no ring on your finger not even a ring from your phone, wondering where he's at, while you look at old pictures of us through your phone

you might say I'm bitter but I swear knowing
you're miserable is sweeter than revenge

She made her love disappear like hocus pocus, maybe I need my glasses and not these glasses so I can focus

You said "put the past behind us" but you kept him on the side, you had me looking forward, so much for things being alright

You said there will always be a place for me in your heart but these nose bleed seats got me feeling like I'm stuck in your head, I think you meant to say there will always be a place for me in your bed unless you're with him and leave me on read

I don't know if I'm falling in love or just stumbling from her intoxicating smile

I know we said we'd take it slow, let's see where it goes, I'll take the high road but we're in the middle of nowhere lost in our phones, standing right next to each other, you said he's just like a brother but he's on you like a uncover

He's so stone cold since he's dated
Medusa, he's a user, boozer, and loser,
why did we let him choose her

I know you got a lot to say but I'm not going to hold my breathe, I'm here sitting on a bar stool wearing a bulletproof vest, taking these shots as they burn my chest

These phone calls got me feeling like this relationship is long distance, we're breaking up, are you still there? Or has my voice become to much to bare

You are not enough, you're worthless, you're a fool for having a heart of gold, I love that you're broken, heart, mind and soul … you're lost and confused, drink those booze to make sense of you, You think you fell in love?? But no … you were tossed, drink that poison and watch time lose track like the light at the end of the tunnel makes you realize how further back she pushed you back, now no one has your back and you can't go back, take those shots like your bullet proof and when that clock hits two know she's not in bed with you, she's in bed with someone new

If only she ran like those tears down her face,
She said everything happened so fast but she
had a hard time saying no to another glass
and a hard time saying no to her past

she threw our future away when our
present wasn't enough of a gift

She hated that his promises and words
were empty, when he was so full of shit

We're on the right track but the light at the end of the tunnel seems to get further away, I'm sorry for the delay but these rainy days just won't go away

You're not a world I choose to call home ...
just one that I choose to conquer

Is it a nightmare if you're all I dream about or is the nightmare waking up without you

A promise ring is nothing more than a participation Trophy

She said "I'm always going be yours even if I'm playing house, just promise me one thing, you'll be as quite as a mouse."

Another year older, as you're staring at your phone, room full of friends but you still feel alone, glass full wine, mind lost in thoughts, heart full of holes maybe it's those shots

This isn't the Love She imagined, He was no Prince Charming, he was a white knight, come to save her ... but the fool didn't know that she was in love with the dragon

This isn't the love she imagined, she kissed
a 100 toads, she even met Prince Charming
once or twice, but she really loved her knights
even if she couldn't remember her nights

We fell in lust ... love was something
our parents did so it wasn't cool

My hope is hanging on to every word
that you say but our plans came up short
like our conversations day to day

I stay away from girls that shoot whiskey, they don't want you to chase them or a chaser

She drinks vodka water just to be clear, she
doesn't want anything sweet not even your talk

I hate when women tell me they miss me like that target on my back was hard to miss, texting me like I owe them one last kiss but if only they would have cared more then they probably would have ended up as a Mrs. (and not a missed call)

She turned the tables just to give me
a taste of my own medicine

It's easier to fall in love with someone new
than to be stuck with the same old boo

Small town girl trying to find herself in this big city but only finds herself a little more lost

I tried to help myself, but the devil grabbed me by my hand and placed the razor to my wrist and whispered in my ear and said "true love doesn't exist"

I'd love to could catch up but she has me wrapped around her finger, I couldn't linger when you had someone else around your ring finger

I'm trying to find the right words to say but the play on my words has me running away, she wanted me out with it but I out witted and got to play her another day

How can I tell you how I feel when the cat gots my tongue and these pills got me numb

You say that I'm amusing like this emotional roller coaster your favorite ride, what's the point of cotton candy? when you can't even swallow your pride

I wish I was boyfriend material but the price of my heart is worthless even though it's gold, I know I need to be confident but I'm confident that this is getting old

My eyes seem to be heavier than my heart, every time I fall I swear I sink into the deepest parts

I hate that when I'm drunk I open up, I vomit nothing but honesty, I'm just another victim of late nights and no sleep I wish I had a Ms. Bo peep to help me count my sheep

I don't want to hurt anyone but I end up hurting everyone including myself -dating in 2018

About the Author

Michael Martinez (born August 31, 1984) is a writer, poet, and observer, growing up in a big city with a small-town mentality in El Paso, Texas. Michael sought to create something that everyone could possibly relate to. Growing up with two sisters and a kid brother, he often saw how men would treated his sisters, wondering how he could help pick up the pieces. While dealing with day to day issues of his own and women that loved him but just couldn't stay in love with him, he found comfort in writing, Michael pulled inspiration from his personal love life and others close to him, sharing the dark side of relationships, substance and alcohol abuse. Michael still lives in his home town of El Paso with his two dogs Dumbo and Turbo, studying martial arts, writing, exploring the paranormal and tuning cars.

INSTAGRAM
@d3feated_

CPSIA information can be obtained
at www.ICGtesting.com
Printed in the USA
FSHW010221180319
56376FS